WRAP IT UP

Creative Gift-Wrapping Ideas

Yoshiko Hase

SHUFUNOTOMO/JAPAN PUBLICATIONS

CONTENTS

PART 1

COMPLETE LESSONS ON WRAPPING TECHNIQUES

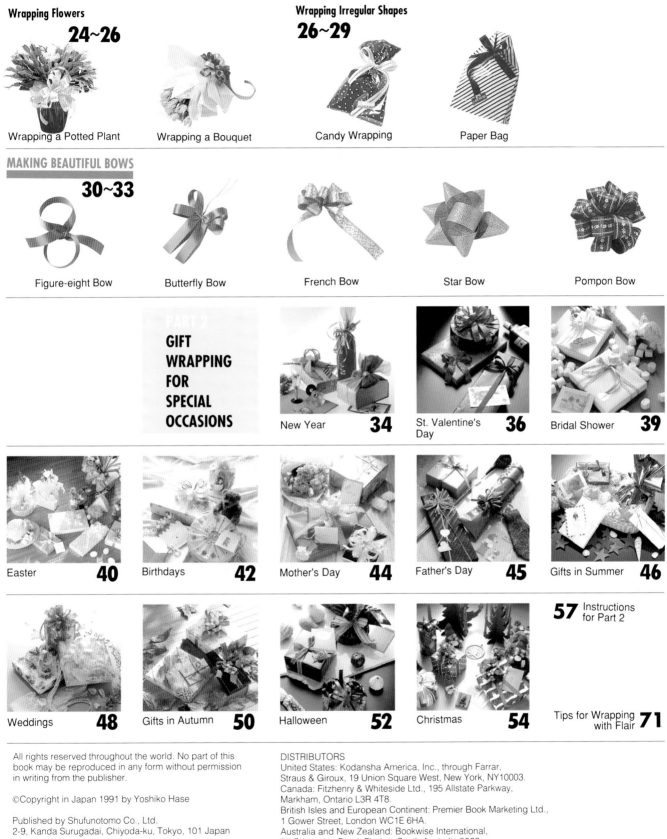

©Copyright in Japan 1991 by Yoshiko Hase

Published by Shufunotomo Co., Ltd.
2-9, Kanda Surugadai, Chiyoda-ku, Tokyo, 101 Japan

ISBN 0-87040-882-2   Printed in Japan

10 9 8 7 6 5 4 3 2 1

DISTRIBUTORS
United States: Kodansha America, Inc., through Farrar, Straus & Giroux, 19 Union Square West, New York, NY10003.
Canada: Fitzhenry & Whiteside Ltd., 195 Allstate Parkway, Markham, Ontario L3R 4T8.
British Isles and European Continent: Premier Book Marketing Ltd., 1 Gower Street, London WC1E 6HA.
Australia and New Zealand: Bookwise International, 54 Crittenden Road, Findon, South Australia 5023.
The Far East and Japan: Japan Publications Trading Co.,Ltd., 1-2-1, Sarugaku-cho, Chiyoda-ku, Tokyo 101.

PART 1

COMPLETE LESSONS ON WRAPPING TECHNIQUES

Basic Ribbon Tying

Diagonal Tie

1. Hold a ribbon about 12" from its end and pass the other end under a corner of a box.

3. Bring the ribbon from under the box and tie it in a bow on the front side.

2. Pull the ribbon over to the front side of the box and pass it again under another corner.

4. Neaten the bow and cut the excess ribbon.

A Bow Variation

An effective new idea but very simple. Just tie separate ribbons in bows around the base of the first bow.

2. Tie a separate ribbon around the base of the bow.

3. Tie it in a bow.

1. Tie a ribbon around a box and tie it in a bow.

4. Tie one more ribbon around the base and cut excess ends off.

Cross Tie

1. Pass a ribbon under the box lengthwise and have it cross on the top side. Pass it again under the box sideways.

2. Bring it to the point on the top side where it crosses.

3. Pass the other end over the cross diagonally and pull the end out from underneath. Tie it in a bow.

Triangle Tie

1. Pass a ribbon twice around a box to make a reverse V-shape.

2. Have it cross with the tail end of the ribbon, making sure the end you passed around the box comes on top of the tail end.

3. Pass the tail end under the ribbon around the box and pull it out. Tie it in a bow.

Basic Wrapping Techniques

There are a number of ways to wrap a parcel, but the methods shown here are the two most basic techniques. Let us go through each step and learn how to measure paper properly and key points in wrapping. Using just the right size paper is the most important factor for best appearance regardless of the technique.

Diagonal Wrapping

Cover each corner of the box one by one while turning it on the diagonal of the paper. This is one of the most familiar wrapping styles encountered daily in Japan. Some people call it "department store wrapping."

How to Wrap Diagonally

1. Place the left front corner of the box on the corner of the paper pointed toward you.

2. Crease a side flap neatly along the edge of the box.

Measure Size of the Paper

Place the box on the diagonal line of the paper. Align the corner of the paper pointed toward you with the left-hand corner of the box. Shift the paper so it projects about 3/4" over the left end.

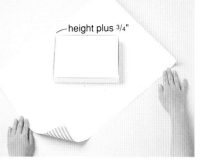

Turn the box once away from you and measure the paper size so the corner shown to be left will not be exposed (height plus 3/4").

3. Fold the side flap up, making sure that the crease you made lines up exactly with the front edge of the box.

Finishing the Final Flap

Crease it along the edge of the box, and then fold under at the crease. The final fold should align neatly with the edge of the box, and also with the side edge of the flap below it.

4. Crease the paper on the upper left corner of the box.

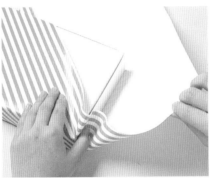

7. Crease the right-hand front corner in the same manner as in (2).

10. Fasten the corner of the paper with a piece of cellophane tape.

For a finishing touch, make a butterfly bow (see P. 31) with a ribbon and fasten it to the parcel with double-sided tape. Fix a seal of your choice to one end of the ribbon.

5. Lifting up your side of the box, fold the paper on the opposite side along the length of the box.

8. Fold the right-hand flap over the box.

6. Lay the box down facing away from you, and make a half turn, making sure that all the folds line up exactly.

9. Lift the paper on the far side of the box and fold it down toward you.

Conventional Wrapping

Conventional wrapping is simple and fail-proof . You place a box squarely in the middle of a piece of paper and fold both side flaps over the edge of the box. This requires a smaller sheet of paper than the diagonal method. It takes just enough to cover the box, with allowance for overlaps.

Measure the Paper Size

1. Place the box in the middle of the paper, allowing an overlap equal to two-thirds of the height of the short end of the box.

2. Fold both sides of the paper over the body of the box and measure the required paper size by allowing 3/4" to 2" for the overlap.

Conventional Wrapping (A)

1. Place the box face down in the middle of the paper and fold both sides over the box. Tape them in place.

2. Push in on both ends and fold the top and bottom flaps along the edges of the box.

3. Fold the edge of the bottom flap over, making sure that the fold comes to the middle of the height of the box.

4. Put double-sided tape on the inside of the folded flap.

5. Fold it up and seal it by pressing gently.

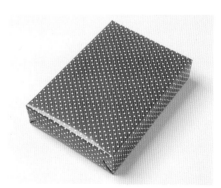

6. Finished view. Paper seam is under the box. Tie a ribbon around the middle of the box and tie it in a bow at the center.

Conventional Wrapping (B)

Fold one end of the paper to form an angle. Place the angle at the front to provide a decorative accent. Place three different ribbons on top of each other and pass them around the middle of the box. Tie them in a bow. Spread them out so you can see each one.

1. Measure the length of the paper by leaving abundant allowance for the overlap.

2. Place the box on the paper with the top facing up. Fold one side of the paper into a desired angle.

3. Fold both sides of the paper over the box, and put the side with folded angle on the top. Shift the paper to find the right spot for the angle. Once you have positioned the angle, tape it.

4. Complete the package by sealing its two ends as described in (A).

Conventional Wrapping (C)

Similar technique as (B) except that an accent is provided by tucking in separate pieces of paper in matching colors.

1. Place the box face up so the end of the inner side flap stops 3/4" to 1 1/4" from the right-hand edge of the box.

2. Fold back the paper at an angle. Wrap the box in a similar manner as in (B). Do not seal the front edge.

3. Take 3 different pieces of paper in desired colors and fold them in half into strips of 1 1/4" to 1 1/2" wide.

4. Tuck the colored papers into the seam at the front and fix them in place with a seal to complete the package.

Conventional Wrapping (D)

Pleats are gathered to add some bulk to the package. Paper with a distinctive pattern is inappropriate because pleating will disturb its continuity. For best effects, choose paper in a solid color or with a plain pattern that can be handled as if it were without a pattern. Tie two different ribbons in different colors around the middle of the box and tie them in a bow.

1. Place the box face up on the paper to determine the desired amount of pleats plus 1½" to 2" overlap.

3. Fold both sides in to cover the box and tape their top edge down.

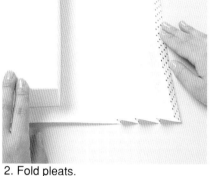

2. Fold pleats.

4. Fold top and bottom flaps and fasten them as outlined in (A).

Tools Necessary for Wrapping

a) Stapler
b) Double-sided tape
c) Cellophane tape
d) Wire
e) Paper knife: For obtaining a cleaner cut on paper than with a regular cutter.
f) Scissors: For ribbon.
g) Cutter: For paper.
h) Adhesive designed for woodwork.
i) Toothbrush: For application of adhesive.
j) Scissors: For wire.
k) Ruler
l) Meltistick: An adhesive for gluegun.
m) Gluegun (See P.70 for how to use.)

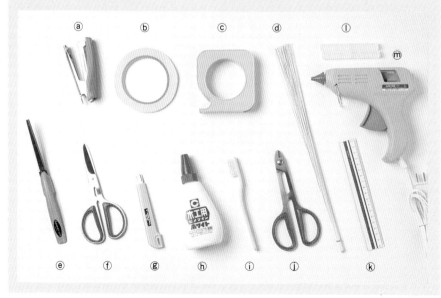

Wrapping Different Shapes

Wrapping a Square Box

2. Lift up a side flap, tucking in the excess paper.

5. Make sure to fold excess paper neatly and tuck it inside the fold.

Square Wrapping (A)

How to wrap: A variation based on diagonal wrapping.
Ribbon: Tie ribbon in a cross around the box and tie it in a bow on the short edge of the box.

3. Do the same for the opposite flap and fix them together with a piece of cellophane tape.

6. Fasten the final flap with a piece of cellophane tape to complete the parcel.

1. Place the box face down in the center of a square sheet of paper. Cut the paper to a size at least 3/4" larger than the height of the box.

4. Fold both corners on the far side in a similar manner.

1. Take a piece of paper that can provide a true square after folding a pleat about 1 1/8" deep. Adjust the width of the pleat according to the box size.

2. Wrap the box in a similar manner as shown in (A).

3. Finished view. When you fold the pleat so its outside fold comes to the exact center of the paper, it appears over the diagonal. Change its location according to your preference.

Square Wrapping (B)

A variation based on (A). Fold a pleat down the center of a sheet of paper and wrap in a similar manner. The pleat can be placed in any location on the box that you like.
Ribbon: Pass a band of ribbon around the parcel and attach a triple figure-eight bow for decoration. You can use the pleat to hold a card in place.

Square Wrapping (C)

A variation based on (A). Stick two colored sheets of paper together and wrap in a similar manner as in (A).
Ribbon: Tie ribbon in a cross around the parcel and decorate it with a triple figure-eight bow.

1. Take two rectangular sheets of paper in different colors.

2. Fold back at a desired angle the edge of the paper you want to have on top.

Square Wrapping (D)

A variation based on (A). Show the edge of the two pieces of paper crossing each other by placing it on the front side of the parcel.

Finishing touch: Take plenty of seals of your choice and stick them at random on the parcel.

1. Fold in about ³/₄" along each edge of the paper and place the box face up in the center.

2. Wrap in a similar manner as in (A).

3. Stick them together with double-sided tape to form a square.

5. Fasten with a piece of cellophane tape.

3. Hold paper in place with double-sided tape.

4. Wrap the box in a similar manner as in (A). Tuck any excess ends of the paper inside.

6. Finished view. Proportion of the two colors can vary with the location of the seam.

Wrapping a Triangular Box

Wrapping an Equilateral Triangle

Wrap the triangle with its center as the place where the paper edges join. When folding in flaps, if you fold by halves taking care not to cause any slack, the folded point of the final flap will come to the exact center of the triangle. Pass a ribbon around the box and tie a bow at the top apex.

1. Place the box in the middle of the paper to decide its height. The end of the paper should come to 1/2" above the center of the box to provide an overlap. The length should be the circumference plus 1 1/2" for the overlap.

2. Align the crease of the fold in step 1 with the corner line at the top apex of the box and tape it in place.

3. Fold the bottom flap up and crease a side flap.

4. Fold the side flap again in half to obtain a 30-degree angle.

5. Fold it down and crease the opposite side.

6. Fold both sides down halfway at the corner angle and pull the flaps down toward you.

7. Fix a seal at the center.

Wrapping an Isosceles Triangle (A)

Wrap the box by placing it so its center lies over the diagonal of the paper. Tuck the excess paper neatly inside the folds during the process.
Finishing touch: Attach a wave bow.

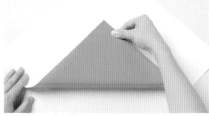

1. Place the box on a square sheet of paper so its center lies over the middle of the diagonal.

2. The far side must come to 3/4" to 1 1/4" above the base.

14

3. Shift the paper so a 3/4" overlap protrudes beyond the top apex. Fold the flap up over the box. Crease.

4. Fold down the side flap and tuck the paper inside along the base of the box.

5. Crease the paper on the other side along the edge of the box and fold it down.

6. Tuck the end of the paper inside so the folded edge lies exactly on the centerline. Fasten with double-sided tape.

Wrapping an Isosceles Triangle (B)

Wrap the box by placing it so its center lies over the diagonal of the paper. Tuck the excess paper neatly inside the folds during the process.
Ribbon: Tie a band of a ribbon around the sides of the triangle and place a pompon bow at the top apex. Attach a seal to fasten the longer end of the ribbon for a finishing touch.

1. Place the box in the middle of a square sheet of paper and measure its size so it equals the height of the box.

2. Place the box face down over the diagonal. Shift the paper so a 3/4" overlap protrudes beyond the top apex.

3. Crease a side flap.

4. Fold the side flap up.

5. Tuck the excess paper inside along the edge of the box and fasten with double-sided tape.

6. Fold the remaining flap in a similar manner.

Wrapping a Cylindrical Box

Cylindrical Wrapping (A)

Make a series of tucks in equal intervals and have them converge for the best results.

Ribbon: Tie ribbon in a cross around the parcel and finish the wrapping by attaching a triple figure-eight bow and a seal.

1. Place the cylinder over the diagonal of a square sheet of paper. Allow overlaps equal to the box's diameter.

2. Rolling it slowly over, make a series of tucks 3/4" to 1 1/4" apart.

3. When you have gone about half the way around the base, fold the paper on the other side up over the cylinder.

4. Fasten it with a piece of cellophane tape.

5. Proceed with the other side by making tucks in a similar manner.

6. Fold the rest of the paper by adjusting its width to that of the cylinder and tucking the excess inside.

7. Fasten the end of the paper with a piece of cellophane tape.

Cylindrical Wrapping (B)

A variation based on (A).
Ribbon: Tie a ribbon in a cross around the parcel and attach double figure-eight bows for decoration. Make three double figure-eight bows in 1", 1/2" and 3/8" ribbon and pile them up in that order.

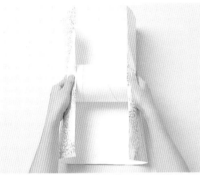

1. Measure paper by allowing 3/4" to 1 1/4" overlap on both ends.

2. Gather a series of tucks on both ends.

3. Fold the rest of the paper in a width corresponding to that of the cylinder.

4. Fasten the paper end with a piece of cellophane tape.

Cylindrical Wrapping (C)

A variation based on (B). Gather tucks only around the base and squeeze paper at the top of the parcel to obtain frills. Adjust the height of the frills according to the overall balance.
Ribbon: Tie a ribbon around the neck where frills are gathered and tie it in a bow.

1. Lay a wider sheet of aluminum foil on top of the paper. Wrap the cylinder with the double layers while making a series of tucks only around its bottom in a similar manner as in (B).

2. Squeeze paper into gathers at the top of the box and tie a ribbon around them.

Cylindrical Wrapping (D)

A variation based on (B). After wrapping a cylinder preliminarily according to the method described in (B), wrap it again with a sheet of patterned cellophane. Use paper in solid color as the inner layer so the pattern on the cellophane stands out.
Ribbon: Tie both ends of the outer wrapping with a ribbon and attach a double figure-eight bow on each end.

1. Roll a cylinder on a sheet of cellophane after wrapping it preliminarily with a sheet of paper.

2. Squeeze both ends into gathers and secure them in place with wire.

Wrapping a Round Box

Round Box Wrapping (A)

This is the basic method for wrapping a round box. The most important point for a neat appearance is to measure the size of the paper accurately.

Ribbon: Tie a ribbon in a cross around the box twice and decorate it with a bow in three different colors.

1. Decide the height of the paper so both ends come to a point exactly 1/4" less than the radius of the box.

2. Allow a 2" overlap. Fold back the end of the paper on the side that comes outside by 3/4" and hold with double-sided tape.

3. Make a regular series of pleats so their folds are at a right angle to the edge of the box.

4. Tuck the last pleat in under the first one.

5. A 3/8" hole will remain at the center, resulting from the difference of 1/4" from the radius of the box in measuring the paper in step 1.

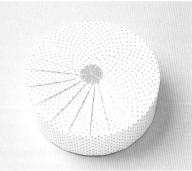

6. Stick a seal at the center.

Round Box Wrapping (B)

Wrap the box preliminarily using method (A). Wind a pleated piece of different paper around it.
Ribbon: Wrap a ribbon around the package in a double row. Fasten a butterfly bow with a gluegun or double-sided tape.

1. The width of the paper should be a little over three times the circumference of the box.

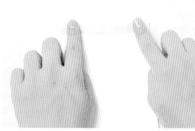

2. Fold back one end of the paper by 3/4".

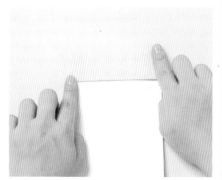

3. Fold the end back again by 1 1/4".

4. Start folding a series of pleats 1/2" apart beginning from the fold made in step 3.

5. Hold pleats in place on the reverse side using cellophane tape.

6. Wind the pleated paper around the preliminarily wrapped box. Trim off any excess.

Application: Hexagonal Box Wrapping

Methods of paper size measurement and wrapping are basically the same as those in (A) but easier because of the straight lines.

1. Fold down the paper neatly along the edges of the box.

2. Crease each side so all the folds meet at the center.

3. Tuck the final fold underneath the first one and affix a seal.

4. Tie a ribbon around the box by passing it on each side crosswise and tie it in a bow.

Round Box Wrapping (C)

A variation of round box wrapping. Use thin soft paper for the best effect because of the large quantity of gathers. Clear material such as cellophane will also look beautiful. Tie ribbon around the gathers and attach a triple figure-eight bow made with 4 strands of ribbon in separate colors.

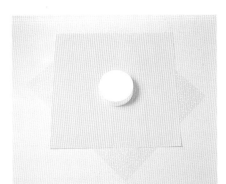

1. With cellophane on the bottom, place two sheets of paper in different colors alternately.

2. Gather the inner sheet toward the center in a similar manner as making tucks.

3. Completion of wrapping with the first sheet.

Round Box Wrapping (D)

A variation of round box wrapping. Place two sheets of paper in different colors side by side and squeeze them to create gathers.
Ribbon: Fasten the paper in place with a wide ribbon and attach a double figure-eight bow made with two strands of a metallic ribbon.

4. Do the same with the outer sheet of cellophane.

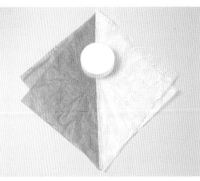

1. Fold and place the sheets of paper along the diagonal with a 1¼" overlap. Tape them in place.

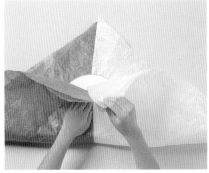

2. Place the box on the overlap and fold the paper in half.

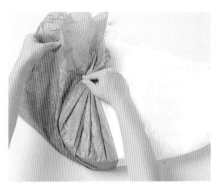

3. Gather the left-hand sheet toward the center.

4. Do the same on the opposite side and squeeze both sheets at the center.

Wrapping a Bottle

Bottle Wrapping (A)

Extra materials: Two-tone paper cords, wire and a seal.

Follow the same method as the candy wrapping. Make gathers at the neck of the bottle. Use clear paper when you want to show the bottle inside.

Ribbon: Tie a ribbon in a bow and insert two-tone paper cords in the middle, then attach a seal as shown by the bottle on the right. Or, as shown below, add a tiny accessory.

1. Measure the paper by placing the bottle in the middle. It should have the same height as the bottle.

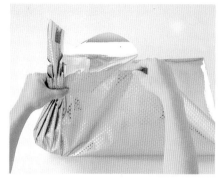

2. Starting from the center, gather the paper on either side into a bunch toward the center at the neck.

3. Fasten it with a piece of wire when it does not gather neatly.

Bottle Wrapping (B)

When the bottle has a round bottom, wrap its base using the same method as in cylindrical wrapping (B).

Ribbon: Fold back a lapel at the top pass a ribbon through it, and tie on bows. Place a figure-eight bow made with two strands of 1/4" ribbon on top of a triple figure-eight bow made with 7/8" ribbon. Hold the longer ends of ribbons in place with a seal.

1. The paper should be 6 3/4" longer than the bottle and half as wide again as the bottle's circumference.

2. Work the base the same as in cylindrical wrapping (B). Fasten paper around bottle's middle with tape.

3. Fold back the top of the parcel by 1 1/4" twice to form the passage for a ribbon.

Bottle Wrapping (C)

Suitable for a wine or champagne bottle. A variation based on (B). A two-inch allowance at the top is sufficient since the paper will not be folded back at the opening.

Ribbon: Tie a ribbon around the middle of the bottle and tie it in a half bow.

1. Fold the paper in half and wrap the bottle in double layers. Proceed with cylindrical wrapping around the base.

2. Fold back the paper diagonally and fasten near the bottom of the package with double-sided tape.

Wrapping Flowers

Wrapping a Potted Plant

Gather paper into pleats evenly along the top of the pot.
Ribbon: Place a French bow at the front. Decide the size of the bow according to the overall balance.

1. Place the pot in the middle of the paper and gather the paper to about 1/4 of the original size. Staple gathers.

2. Make gathers at 4 or 5 spots around the pot.

1. Lay two sheets of paper on top of each other, one slightly off center. Place the basket in the center.

2. Gather them in a bunch at each side of the basket.

Wrapping a Flower Basket

The point is to enhance the total look of flowers already arranged. Use muted wrapping so the flower colors appear even more attractive.

3. Fasten gathers together using a stapler.

4. Do the same on the opposite side and arrange overall shapes for a pleasant appearance.

Ribbon: Tie a ribbon around the spots stapled together and tie a triple figure-eight bow at each spot. Place a card, etc., for additional decoration.

Wrapping a Flower

Standard method for a rose about 16" tall. Wrap the cut end of its stalk with a wet piece of tissue paper or cotton and cover it with aluminium foil.

Ribbon: Pass a ribbon around the middle of the package and tie a triple figure-eight bow.

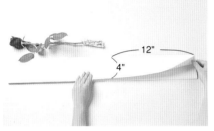

1. Take a piece of paper 16" in width. Fold it in four. Cut the four thicknesses to the height of the flower plus 3 times the width of the strip (12").

2. Fold back the extra length.

3. Fold it again at the corner in a triangle to produce a right angle.

4. Next, fold it down toward the reverse side.

5. Fold its end diagonally to form a triangle.

6. Tuck the triangular flap underneath the opposite flap.

7. Place the flower inside.

Ribbon: Wrap a ribbon around the bottom of the bouquet and tie a French bow in place at the front. Decide on the size of the bow according to overall balance.

Wrapping Irregular Shapes

Wrapping a Bouquet

Put flowers together in a bundle. Cover their cut ends with aluminium foil after wrapping them with wet pieces of tissue paper or cotton. Since two layers of paper in different colors are used, choose an effective color combination.

1. The paper should be twice as tall as the flowers. Lay one sheet of paper on top of the other, off-center.

2. Pull flowers down slightly toward you and fold the inner sheet up.

3. Fold both sides of the inner sheet in.

4. Fold the outer sheet similarly, tucking excess paper inside.

5. Squeeze the paper into gathers to handle excessive outward expansion.

Candy Wrapping

When wrapping a muffler or scarf, fold it beforehand. An accessory should be preliminarily wrapped with a thin piece of paper.
Ribbon: Tie a ribbon around the opening and tie it in a bow. Hold its longer end in place with a seal.

1. Fold the article to be placed inside a little smaller than a half of the width and a quarter of the height of the paper.

Folded Triangle

Appropriate for small and flat articles such as an accessory or handkerchief. Use thick, firm paper.
Ribbon: Pass a ribbon in a cross and once again around the middle of the package and tie it in a bow at the center.

4. Turn the folded end back so the fold in step 3 lines up exactly with the lower edge of the quadruple thickness.

2. Place two sheets of paper under the article with the cellophane on the bottom. Fold in both sides and tape.

1. Fold in the top and bottom sides of the paper so both ends meet at the centerline.

5. Repeat the procedure and form an equilateral triangle. Fold the shorter side of the remaining paper at 60°.

3. Fold them in half. The resultant fold constitutes the bottom of the package.

2. Fold it again to make a quadruple thickness.

6. Tuck the remaining flap inside the triangle and crease the corner.

4. Squeeze below the opening to form gathers.

3. Turn its end back to create a 60-degree angle at the upper corner.

7. Open the triangle and place an article inside. Fold it again to complete the package.

Shirt-shaped Wrapping

Appropriate for a flat article. The paper size given here is suitable for an article about 4" square. When you want to change the size of the package, try folding it using newspaper, etc. Use firm paper. Place the article inside after shaping the shirt.

Finishing touch: Pass a ribbon under the collar and tie it in a bow. Affix a seal of your choice.

2. Fold in top and bottom sides of the paper so both ends meet at the centerline.

4. Turn the paper over and fold the other end back twice by 1". The resultant lapel will hold the ribbon.

1. Cut the paper to a 22" x 12" rectangle. Fold back one of the shorter sides from the end by 3".

3. Turn back both corners of the folded end about 60 degrees to create sleeves.

5. Turn it over again and fold back both corners diagonally to make both apexes meet at the center joint.

6. Fold back the end with sleeves and tuck it under the collar.

7. Align the center properly and crease the bottom neatly.

Paper Bag

Appropriate for a bulky article or for placing a combination of articles inside. To decide the paper size, try folding the bag with old wrapping paper of a suitable size to make a paper pattern. Ribbon: Pass a ribbon through the lapel folded at the opening and tie it in a bow. Fix the longer end with a seal.

1. Fold back one of the longer sides of the paper from the end by a quarter of the length.

2. Fold back the opposite side and have it overlap with the other side by 1/4" to 1/2". Affix double-sided tape.

3. Fold up by the width of the base plus a 1/4" margin for pasting up.

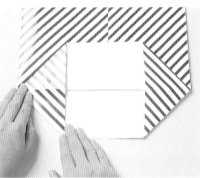

4. Open up the base flap you just folded and fold both ends in a triangle.

5. Fold down the top flap in the middle to obtain half the width of the base. Fasten both corners with tape .

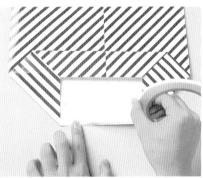

6. Fold up the bottom flap similarly and fasten it onto the opposite side with double-sided tape.

7. This completes the bag.

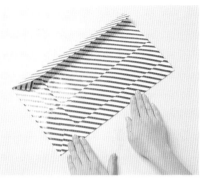

8. Crease firmly along both sides of the bag to provide gussets.

9. Using the existing creases, refold them to indicate those to be indented from the reverse side.

10. Fold down the opening toward the reverse side twice by 1" and fold in both corners diagonally.

Making Beautiful Bows

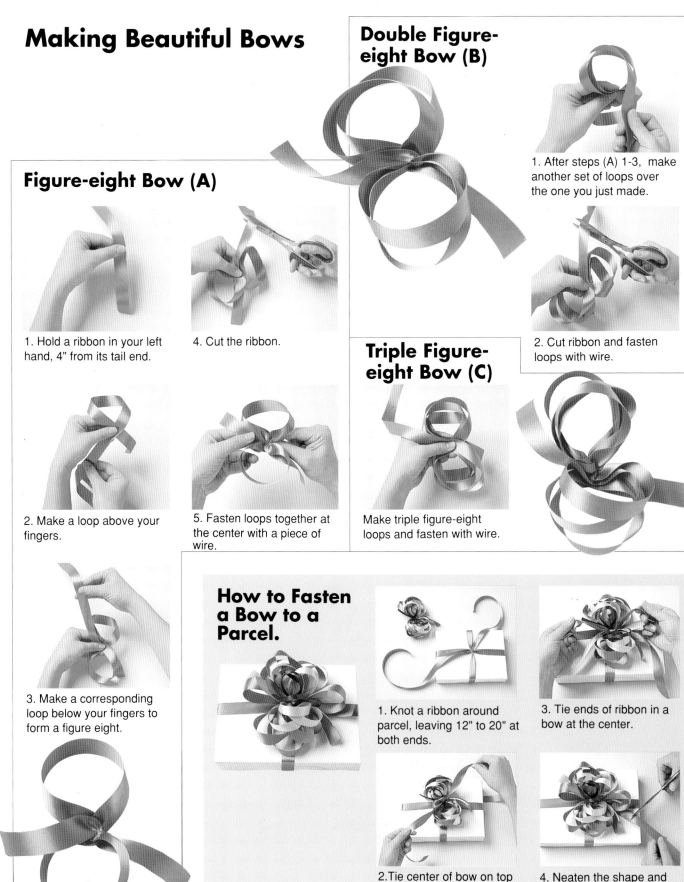

Figure-eight Bow (A)

1. Hold a ribbon in your left hand, 4" from its tail end.

2. Make a loop above your fingers.

3. Make a corresponding loop below your fingers to form a figure eight.

4. Cut the ribbon.

5. Fasten loops together at the center with a piece of wire.

Double Figure-eight Bow (B)

1. After steps (A) 1-3, make another set of loops over the one you just made.

2. Cut ribbon and fasten loops with wire.

Triple Figure-eight Bow (C)

Make triple figure-eight loops and fasten with wire.

How to Fasten a Bow to a Parcel.

1. Knot a ribbon around parcel, leaving 12" to 20" at both ends.

2. Tie center of bow on top of the knot.

3. Tie ends of ribbon in a bow at the center.

4. Neaten the shape and trim off excess ends.

1. Make a triple figure-eight bow with a wide ribbon. Take another ribbon of an intermediate width and make a smaller triple figure-eight immediately over the one just made.

2. Make an even smaller figure eight over them with a narrow ribbon.

3. Tie a metallic ribbon around the center, leaving at both ends about 12". Fasten eights in the middle with a piece of wire.

4. Run the back of the scissors down the length of the metallic ribbon, pressing very hard as you do so, causing it to curl.

Atelier Majo Bow (D)

Butterfly Bow

1. Make a loop above your fingers as shown.

2. Make another loop below your fingers. Cut here if you want a single bow.

3. Turn the ribbon over and make a loop to the left of the loop made in step 1.

4 Bring the ribbon around toward your side and cut it.

5. Fasten the center with wire.

How to Fasten with Wire

1. Pass wire around a bow in the middle, holding both ends firmly in your right hand.

2. Cause ribbon to form gathers at the center by pulling both bow and wire away from each other.

3. Twist the wire by turning the bow 2 or 3 times to complete fastening.

4. Cut wire close to the bow if you do not use it to fasten the bow to your parcel.

Wave Bow

French Bow

1. Make a loop at the end of a ribbon. This represents the center loop of the bow.

2. Fold the ribbon under the loop, going back and forth twice. Shift the length between folds equally on both sides as you do so.

3. Cut the ribbon and fasten the bow at the center with a stapler.

1. Make a loop at the end of a ribbon. This represents the center loop of the bow.

2. Cause the ribbon to make a half turn by twisting it under the loop's center.

3. Loop the ribbon back and twist to make another half turn.

4. Loop it back again and twist it at the center.

5. Make the next loop on the left side of the loop in step 3.

6. Make the next loop on the right side of the loop in step 4.

7. Make required number of loops. Nine loops are made in this example.

8. Finally, make a large ring and cut the ribbon.

9. Pass wire around the center of the bow to hold loops together.

10. Cut the large ring in half to use as hangings. Adjust their length as you like.

Note: Suitable for a ribbon with a distinction between right and wrong sides. Make the bow so the right side is always facing outside.

Pompon Bow

1. Wind a ribbon 4 to 8 times in a circle of the size bow you want.

5. Pass wire around the notches.

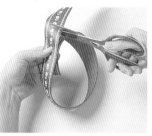

2. Cut the ribbon, having added about 2" allowance for overlap.

6. Pull an inner loop toward the outside.

3. Flatten the circle and cut a small notch on both sides.

7. By holding the center firmly with your left hand, pull the loop out completely.

4. Open the circle and have the notches match in the center.

8. Pull loops out from either side alternately and fluff nicely.

Star Bow

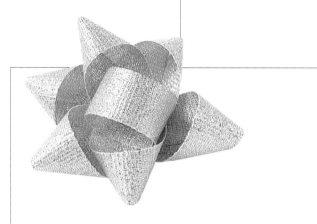

1. Make a triangular loop in a ribbon above your fingers.

4. Make 5 or 6 loops by shifting their positions to form a star shape.

2. Make a corresponding triangular loop below your fingers. Bring the ribbon up.

5. Make a small loop at the center and cut the ribbon.

3. Make a triangular loop on the left side of the top loop.

6. Fasten loops together at the center with a stapler.

PART 2

GIFT WRAPPING FOR SPECIAL OCCASIONS

ST. VALENTINE'S DAY

13

14

15

16

BRIDAL SHOWER

EASTER

22

23

25

BIRTHDAYS

29

31

Hi

30

MOTHER'S DAY

FATHER'S DAY

GIFTS IN SUMMER

WEDDINGS

GIFTS IN AUTUMN

50

51

52

HALLOWEEN

55

56

57

Happy
Halloween!

CHRISTMAS

61

62

INSTRUCTIONS
FOR PART 2
(P.34~P.56)

1

Use diagonal wrapping.
Ribbon: Tie a ribbon in a cross around the parcel and attach figure-eight bows.

Make a triple figure-eight bow with a 1/8" ribbon over a triple figure-eight bow with a 1" ribbon.

2

Use conventional wrapping (A) for this box.
Ribbon: Tie ribbon around parcel. Make a triple figure-eight bow with a 1/2" ribbon, a double figure-eight bow with a 1/4" ribbon, and a triple figure-eight bow with double strands of a two-tone paper cord. Attach them in that order.

3

Use hexagonal box wrapping, an application of round box wrapping (A).
Ribbon: Pass a ribbon around the box on each side crosswise and tie it in a bow. Arrange two-tone paper cords in a desired shape in a similar manner as in making a figure-eight bow. Tuck the paper cords under the ribbon for additional decoration.

4

An application of conventional wrapping (A). Fold back the end of the paper that protrudes outside. Position paper seam off center and on the front side.

Ribbon: Tie a ribbon in a cross around the parcel and tie it in a bow over a figure-eight bow made with paper cords. Make the figure-eight bow with 15 strands of two-tone paper cords.

6

Use conventional wrapping (A) for this box.

Ribbon: Paste two sheets of Japanese paper in different colors together and fold them up to the width of the parcel. Wrap the parcel with the folded paper and tie it in a half bow like a scarf.

5

An application of cylindrical wrapping (C). Wrap a bottle by placing it diagonally on two sheets of paper.

Ribbon: Wrap a ribbon around the neck of the bottle and tie figure-eight bows and two-tone paper cords in place. Make a triple figure-eight bow with a 1/4" ribbon, a double figure-eight bow with a 1/8" ribbon and a single figure-eight bow with two strands of metallic ribbon and pile them up in that order. Run the back of scissors down the ends of the metallic ribbon, pressing very hard, to cause them to curl.

7

Use diagonal wrapping.

Ribbon: Tie a ribbon in a cross around the parcel and tie it in a bow.

8

Use conventional wrapping (B) for this box.
Ribbon: Pass a ribbon in a band around the parcel lengthwise and tie it in a bow. Add an accessory of your choice for decoration.

Use diagonal wrapping. Finishing touch: Stick a butterfly bow in place with double-sided tape.

11

9

Use conventional wrapping (A) for this box.
Ribbon: Tie a ribbon in a cross around the parcel and attach a triple figure-eight bow.

10

Use round box wrapping (A) for this type of box.
Finishing touch: Fasten a pompon bow at the center.

12

Use diagonal wrapping.
Ribbon: Tie a ribbon in a cross around the parcel and tie it in a bow.

13

Use square wrapping (A).
Ribbon: Tie a ribbon in a cross around a box and tie it in a bow.

14

Use diagonal wrapping.
Ribbon: Tie a ribbon in a cross around a box and tie it in a bow.

16

Use conventional wrapping (A) for this box.
Ribbon: Pass a ribbon around a box diagonally twice and tie it in a bow over an accessory. Make the accessory by attaching a heart-shaped decoration to an end of colored wire. Complete the parcel by adding lacey paper or a card as a finishing touch.

Use conventional wrapping (D).
Ribbon: Tie a ribbon around a box diagonally twice and attach a triple figure-eight bow. Complete the parcel by tucking decoration such as lacey paper in pleats on the front side.

15

17

Use diagonal wrapping.
Ribbon: Tie a ribbon in a cross around a box and tie it in a bow.

18

Use a variation of round box wrapping.
Cover the box with a sheet of paper and squeeze it into gathers at both ends.
Ribbon: Tie a ribbon in a knot around the gathers and tie it in a bow over a triple figure-eight bow made with a 1" ribbon.

20

Use round box wrapping (C).
Ribbon: Tie a ribbon around the gathers at the center to hold them together and tie a triple figure-eight bow in place.

19

Use square wrapping (A).
Ribbon: Tie two strands of ribbons in different colors in a cross around the box and tie them in a bow. Spread them out so they look attractive and fasten a seal on the edge of one of the loose ends.

21

Use diagonal wrapping.
Ribbon: Tie a ribbon in a cross around a box and tie it in a bow.

22

Use diagonal wrapping.
Ribbon: Pass a ribbon in the middle of a box lengthwise twice and tie it in a knot. Attach figure-eight bows on the knot. Make a quadruple figure-eight bow with a 1" ribbon and a triple figure-eight bow with a 1/4" ribbon and pile them on top of each other. Spread the ribbon around the box on both sides and neaten the appearance.

Use conventional wrapping (B) for this box.
Ribbon: Tie a ribbon in a cross around a box and fasten a triple figure-eight bow in place. Attach small flowers for additional decoration while maintaining overall balance.

23

Use square wrapping (A).
Ribbon: Tie a ribbon in a double cross around the box and tie figure-eight bows in place at the center. Make a double figure-eight bow with a 1/8" ribbon on top of a quadruple figure-eight bow with a 1" ribbon.

26

Use equilateral triangle wrapping.
Ribbon: Use two strands at all times. Pass the ribbon in a band around the sides of the triangular box and tie a quadruple figure-eight bow in place.

24

27

First wrap the box using the method in round box wrapping (A). Next, place the box in the middle of a sheet of cellophane and squeeze it into gathers at the center.

25

Use application of conventional wrapping (A).
Wrap the box after attaching a pleated sheet of colored paper with double-sided tape on the wrapping paper.
Ribbon: Tie a ribbon in a cross around the box and attach two triple figure-eight bows in different colors, one on top of the other.

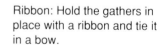

Ribbon: Hold the gathers in place with a ribbon and tie it in a bow.

28

Use round box wrapping (A).
Ribbon: Pass a ribbon in a band around the side of the box and tie it in a bow.

31

Use diagonal wrapping.
Ribbon: Pass a ribbon across four corners of the box and attach a double figure-eight bow.

29

Use square wrapping (A).
Ribbon: Tie a ribbon in a band around the middle of the box and tie it in a bow.

30

Use diagonal wrapping.
Ribbon: Tie a ribbon in a cross around the box and tie it in a bow.

32

Use square wrapping (A).
Wrap the box with a sheet of paper in a metallic color and wrap it again with a sheet of cellophane.
Ribbon: Tie a ribbon in a cross around the box and tie it in a bow. Leave one end of the ribbon long.

33

Use diagonal wrapping for the larger box and conventional wrapping (A) for the smaller one.
Ribbon: Place the smaller box on top of the larger one. Tie a ribbon in a cross around them and tie it in a bow. Tie it in a bow twice at the base of the first bow.

35

Use square wrapping (A).
Ribbon: Tie a ribbon around the box and tie it in a bow.

36

Fold pleats around the base in the same manner as in bottle wrapping (B). Fold the top toward the reverse side and hold it in place with a piece of cellophane tape.
Ribbon: Tie a ribbon around the neck of the bottle and fasten figure-eight bows. Make a figure-eight bow with two strands of metallic ribbon and place it on top of a triple figure-eight bow made with a 1/2" ribbon. Leave all of the ribbon ends long. Wind the 1/2" ribbon around the bottle and down its height diagonally and hold it in place with double-sided tape. Cause the ribbon to curl by running the back of the scissors down its length, pressing very hard.

34

Use conventional wrapping (A) for this box.
Ribbon: Tie a ribbon in a cross around the box and attach a bow

37

Use conventional wrapping (A) for this box.
Ribbon: Use different colored ribbons in two strands. Tie ribbons in a cross around the box and attach a quadruple figure-eight bow. Spread out ribbons around the box for optimum appearance. Affix a seal to hold ribbon ends in place.

Use conventional wrapping. Ribbon: Tie a ribbon in a cross around the box and tie it in a bow. Twine one of its ends around the knot and pull the loops of the bow up.

40

Use diagonal wrapping.
Ribbon: Tie a ribbon in a band around the box both horizontally and vertically and tie each band in a bow.

38

Use square wrapping (A).
Ribbon: Pass a ¼" ribbon in a band around the sides of the box first and tie it in a cross around it, attaching figure-eight bows. Place a double figure-eight bow made with metallic ribbon on top of a triple figure-eight bow in a ¾" ribbon. Cause both ends of the metallic ribbon to curl by running the back of the scissors down the length of the ribbon, pressing very hard.

41

Use conventional wrapping (A) for this box.
Ribbon: Lay one ribbon on top of another in a different color, using them in two strands at all times. Pass them in a band down the length of the box first and then around two corners diagonally. Tie them in a bow. Pass ribbons under the knot of the bow and tie them again in a bow to make double bows.

42

Use bottle wrapping (A).
Ribbon: Use three strands
of ribbons in different colors
and tie them in a bow
around the neck of the
bottle.

45

Use square wrapping (A).
Ribbon: Tie a ribbon in a
cross and tie it in a knot.
Cut ribbon ends. Fasten a
pompon bow to the knot
with wire for decoration.

43

Use round box wrapping (A).
Ribbon: Pass a ribbon
around the box three times
making an even interval so
the knot will come to the
exact center of the top of
the box and tie a French
bow in place at the center.

46

Use conventional wrapping
(A) for this box.
Ribbon: Place a piece of
lacey paper over the box.
Pass a ribbon in a cross
around the box and over the
lacey paper. Pass the
ribbon again in a band
horizontally. Attach figure-
eight bows. Make a figure-
eight bow with double
strands of metallic ribbon
and place it on top of a
quadruple figure-eight bow
made with a lacey ribbon.
Leave both ends of the
metallic ribbon long and curl
them with a scissors blade.

44

Use diagonal wrapping.
Ribbon: Tie a ribbon in a
cross around the box .
Make a triple figure-eight
bow with a 1" ribbon, a
quintuple and quadruple
figure-eight bow each with
1/8" ribbon and attach them
on top of each other in that
order.

47

Use square wrapping (A). Finishing touch: Attach a French bow with double-sided tape.

50

Use diagonal wrapping. Ribbon: Tie a ribbon diagonally around the box twice and tie it in a bow.

48

Use diagonal wrapping. Ribbon: Tie a ribbon around the middle of the box and fasten a French bow in place. Stick a seal over the longer end of the ribbon.

51

Use square wrapping (A). Ribbon: Tie a ribbon in a cross around the box and fasten figure-eight bows. Make a double figure-eight bow with 1/2" ribbon and place it on top of a triple figure-eight bow made with 3/4" ribbon.

49

Use square wrapping (A). Ribbon: Tie a ribbon in a cross around the box and attach a ninefold figure-eight bow.

52

Use diagonal wrapping.
Ribbon: Tie a ribbon in a cross around the box and tie it in a bow. Add an accessory for decoration if you wish.

53

Use the same method as in cylindrical wrapping (C) except that you use a single sheet of paper.
Ribbon: Tie a ribbon around the opening in a knot and fasten figure-eight bows for decoration. Make a figure-eight bow with 3/4" ribbon, a triple figure-eight bow with 1" ribbon, and another figure-eight bow with 3/4" ribbon. Pile them on top of each other in that order.

55

Use square wrapping (A).
Ribbon: Tie a ribbon around the box and tie it in a bow. Add an accessory of your choice for additional decoration.

54

Use the same method as in cylindrical wrapping (C). Wrap the box by placing the inner sheet of aluminium foil diagonally over the outer sheet of paper.
Ribbon: Tie a ribbon around the opening in a knot and fasten a triple figure-eight bow in place. Add any seal or accessory of your choice for a finishing touch.

56

Use round box wrapping (C). Use a single sheet of paper.
Ribbon: Tie a ribbon around the opening and tie it in a bow.

57

Use round box wrapping (A).
Ribbon: Place two different colored ribbons on top of each other and pass them around the box three times as you do when you tie them in a cross, making sure you place them at equal intervals. Fasten figure-eight bows in place. Make a quadruple figure-eight bow with $3/4"$ ribbon and a triple one with $1/2"$ ribbon separately and pile them on top of each other.

59

Use square wrapping (A).
Ribbon: Tie a ribbon around the box and tie it in a bow.

60

Use round box wrapping (A).
Ribbon: Tie a ribbon in a cross around the box twice and fasten figure-eight bows in place at the center. Make a double figure-eight bow with two strands of $1/8"$ ribbon on top of a triple figure-eight bow made with $1 1/2"$ ribbon.

58

Use cylindrical wrapping (B).
Ribbon: Tie a ribbon around the box and tie it in a bow. Stick on seals.

61

Use diagonal wrapping.
Ribbon: Tie a ribbon around the box and tie it in a bow. Stick on seals.

Use conventional wrapping (A) for this box.
Ribbon: Pass a ribbon in a V-shape around the box and fasten on figure-eight bows. Make a figure-eight bow with two strands of a metallic ribbon on top of a quadruple figure-eight bow made with 3/4" ribbon. Run the back of the scissors down the length of the metallic ribbon ends, pressing very hard to cause them to curl.

62

63

Use hexagonal wrapping, which is an application of round box wrapping.
Ribbon: Pass a ribbon around each side of the box and tie a knot at the center. Fasten a triple figure-eight bow in place.

65

Use diagonal wrapping.
Ribbon: Pass a ribbon around two corners of the box diagonally and fasten a quadruple figure-eight bow in place. Stick on a seal.

64

Use diagonal wrapping.
Ribbon: Tie a ribbon in a cross around the box and tie it in a bow.

How to use a gluegun

Place Meltistick, an adhesive, inside the gluegun and stick your accessory on the package where you want it. It will be secured completely in place when the adhesive cools.

Tips for Wrapping with Flair

Before beginning to wrap a present, think about the person who is going to receive it. What style would please that person the most? Choose a style that fits the personality of the recipient.

The secret to achieving the effect you want lies in how the paper and the ribbon are coordinated.

When using solid paper, you have a choice of ribbon in a similar color or ribbon in a contrasting color. If you choose a similar color, the effect will be soft and restrained. If you choose a contrasting color, the result will be a bolder appearance.

When using patterned paper, if you select ribbon that matches the palest color in the paper, the effect will be muted. If you select ribbon that matches a strong color in the paper, the effect will be bold.

To create an interesting and unusual effect, use two or more kinds of paper for the same package. If you use similar colors, the effect will be muted; contrasting colors will result in a bold, eye-catching package.

Ribbons come in many kinds, shapes, and widths. Choose ribbon that will harmonize well with the contents of your package, as well as with the wrapping paper.

Ribbon size should also harmonize with box size. If you are using a large box, use wide ribbon. If only narrow ribbon is available when you are wrapping a large box, then use two or three strands at the same time.

It's best to keep a varied assortment of paper and ribbon at home, if you want to wrap packages that create different moods. On the other hand, you may prefer to use always the same paper and ribbon, so that when people see presents wrapped with these, they will know that the giver is you.

Other handy items to keep at home are interesting seals and unusual objects to affix to packages. Perhaps seashells you found on the beach, or acorns or pine-cones. Tiny toys or decorative objects to go on children's present are always welcome. A teddy bear, or a witch to use at Halloween.

Decorate your packages with items that are seasonal. In spring, use fresh spring flowers; in autumn, a beautiful leaf. Berries can be used, but not the kind that stain.

When wrapping flowers, it is thoughtful to use ribbon that will not bleed if it gets wet.

Use your imagination, but equally important, use your heart. The best present is one whose contents and wrapping show an understanding and appreciation of the person to whom you are giving it.

Lastly, always remember that when someone cares enough about you to give you a present, acknowledge their kindness by sending a thank-you note promptly.

Yoshiko Hase is chairwoman of the board of the Gift Wrapping Art Academy and president of Atelier Majo. Hase has been very active in the fields of gift-wrapping and making ribbon flowers. Her books in Japanese include:

Published by Shufunotomo
"Ribbon Art Flowers"
"Ribbons for All Seasons"
"Wrapping Text"

Published by Nihon Vogue
"Ribbon Art for Beginners"
"Ribbon Art" Parts 1-4,
"Gift Ribbon Book"
"100 Wrapping Ideas"
"Door Wreaths"
"Play with Ribbons"
"Gift Wrapping"

Published by Seibundo Shinko-sha
"Present Ideas"
"Flower Wrapping
"New Flower Wrapping"
"Ribbon Art"
"Book of Wreath Ideas"

Published by Gakken
"Flowers and Presents"

Published by Boutique-sha
"Ribbons for Christmas"

Published by Aoyama
"Book about Presents"